W9-AIA-154

SIOUX
History and Culture

Helen Dwyer and D. L. Birchfield

Consultant Robert J. Conley
Sequoyah Distinguished Professor at Western Carolina University

Gareth Stevens
Publishing

Please visit our website, **www.garethstevens.com.** For a free color catalog of all our high-quality books, call toll free 1-800-542-2595 or fax 1-877-542-2596.

Library of Congress Cataloging-in-Publication Data

Birchfield, D. L., 1948-
Sioux history and culture / D. L. Birchfield and Helen Dwyer.
    p. cm. — (Native American library)
Includes index.
ISBN 978-1-4339-6682-8 (pbk.)
ISBN 978-1-4339-6683-5 (6-pack)
ISBN 978-1-4339-6680-4 (library binding)
1. Dakota Indians—History. 2. Dakota Indians—Social life and customs. I. Dwyer, Helen. II. Title.
E99.D1B58 2012
978.004'975243—dc22

                    2011016307

New edition published in 2012 by
Gareth Stevens Publishing
111 East 14th Street, Suite 349
New York, NY 10003

First edition published 2005 by Gareth Stevens Publishing

Copyright © 2012 Gareth Stevens Publishing

Produced by Discovery Books
Project editor: Helen Dwyer
Designer and page production: Sabine Beaupré
Photo researchers: Tom Humphrey and Helen Dwyer
Maps: Stefan Chabluk

Photo credits: AP/Wide World Photos: pp. 16 (top), 26, 31, 38, 39; Corbis: pp. 13, 35 (Marilyn Angel Wynn/Native Stock Pictures), 37 (Maggie Steber/ National Geographic Society); © Kevin Locke: p. 33; Library of Congress: pp. 18, 22 (bottom); © Mary Annette Pember: pp. 32, 36; National Park Service, Little Bighorn Battlefield National Monument: pp. 14 (bottom), 15, 16 (bottom), 17; North Wind Picture Archives: pp. 11, 14 (top), 19, 20, 21, 22 (top), 23; Shutterstock: pp. 5 (Bryan Brazil), 28 (anotherlook), 29 (Shawn Hempel); SuperStock, Inc.: pp. 12, 24, 27; © Tiffany Midge: p. 34; Wikimedia: pp. 7 (Karl Bodmer), 8 (Hermann Heyn).

Printed in the United States of America

CPSIA compliance information: Batch #CW12GS: For further information contact Gareth Stevens, New York, New York at 1-800-542-2595.

CONTENTS

Words that appear in the glossary are printed in **boldface** type the first time they appear in the text.

INTRODUCTION

The Sioux are a people who mainly live in North and South Dakota, Minnesota, and Montana. They are just one of the many groups of Native Americans who live today in North America. There are well over five hundred Native American tribes in the United States and more than six hundred in Canada. At least three million people in North America consider themselves to be Native Americans. But who are Native Americans, and how do the Sioux fit into the history of North America's Native peoples?

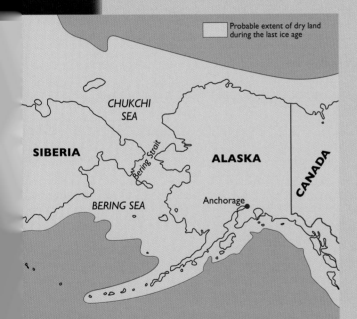

Siberia (Asia) and Alaska (North America) are today separated by an area of ocean named the Bering Strait. During the last ice age, the green area on this map was at times dry land. The Asian ancestors of the Sioux walked from one continent to the other.

THE FIRST IMMIGRANTS

Native Americans are people whose **ancestors** settled in North America thousands of years ago. These ancestors probably came from eastern parts of Asia. Their **migrations** probably occurred during cold periods called **ice ages.** At these times, sea levels were much lower than they are now. The area between northeastern Asia and Alaska was dry land, so it was possible to walk between the continents.

Scientists know that these migrations must have taken place more than twelve thousand years ago. Around that time, water levels rose and covered the land between Asia and the Americas.

The Cliff Palace at Mesa Verde, Colorado, is the most spectacular example of Native American culture that survives today. It consists of more than 150 rooms and pits built around A.D. 1200 from sandstone blocks.

By around ten thousand years ago, the climate had warmed and was similar to conditions today. The first peoples in North America moved around the continent in small groups, hunting wild animals and collecting a wide variety of plant foods. Gradually these groups spread out and lost contact with each other. They developed separate **cultures** and adopted lifestyles that suited their **environments**.

SETTLING DOWN

Although many tribes continued to gather food and hunt or fish, some Native Americans began to live in settlements and grow crops. Their homes ranged from underground pit houses and huts of mud and thatch to dwellings in cliffs. By 3500 B.C., a plentiful supply of fish in the Pacific Ocean and in rivers had enabled people to settle in large coastal villages from Alaska to Washington State. In the deserts of Arizona more than two thousand years later, farmers constructed hundreds of miles of **irrigation** canals to carry water to their crops.

In the Ohio River valley between 700 B.C. and A.D. 500, people of the Adena and Hopewell cultures built clusters of large burial mounds, such as the Serpent Mound in Ohio, which survives today. In the Mississippi **floodplains**, the Native peoples formed complex societies. They created mud and thatch temples on top of flat earth pyramids. Their largest town, Cahokia, in Illinois, contained more than one hundred mounds and may have been home to thirty thousand people.

CONTACT WITH EUROPEANS

Around A.D. 1500, European ships reached North America. The first explorers were the Spanish. Armed with guns and riding horses, they took over land and forced the Native Americans to work for them. The Spanish were followed by the British, Dutch, and French, who were looking for land to settle and for opportunities to trade.

When Native Americans met these Europeans they came into contact with diseases, such as smallpox and measles, that they had never experienced before. At least one half of all Native Americans, and possibly many more than that, were unable to overcome these diseases and died.

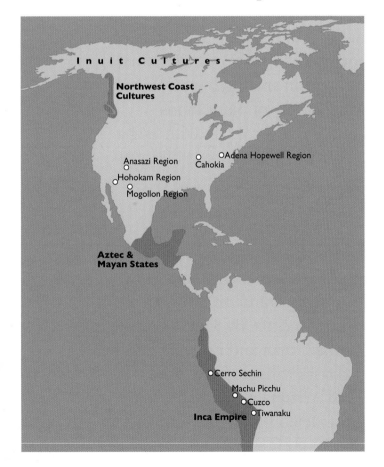

This map highlights some of the main early American cultures.

This illustration of a Sioux chief's funeral platform was painted by Karl Bodmer in the 1840s. Bodies were wrapped and placed on a shelf high above the ground, out of reach of wild animals.

Guns were also disastrous for Native Americans. At first, only the Europeans had guns, which enabled them to overcome native peoples in fights and battles. Eventually, Native American groups obtained guns and used them in conflicts with each other. When the Ojibwe people obtained guns from the French they used their new weapons to drive the Sioux tribes westward, out of their woodland homes in the Mississippi River Valley and onto the Great Plains of present-day Wyoming, North and South Dakota, and western Minnesota. Many Native American groups were also forced to take sides and fight in wars between the French and British.

Horses, too, had a big influence in Native American lifestyles, especially for tribes like the Sioux on the Great Plains. People were able to travel greater distances and began to hunt buffalo on horseback. Soon horses became central to Plains trade and social life.

At the end of the 1700s, people of European descent began to migrate over the Appalachian Mountains, looking for new land to farm and exploit. By the middle of the nineteenth century, they had reached the west coast of North America. This expansion was disastrous for Native Americans. The Sioux went to war with the United States in the 1850s, 1860s, and 1870s, but were finally forced to surrender in 1877.

RESERVATION LIFE

Many peoples were pressured into moving onto **reservations** to the west. The biggest of these reservations later became the U.S. state of Oklahoma. Native Americans who tried to remain in their homelands were attacked and defeated.

New laws in the United States and Canada took away most of the control Native Americans had over their lives. They were expected to give up their cultures and adopt the ways and habits of white Americans. It became a crime to practice their traditional religions. Children were taken from their homes and placed in **boarding schools**, where they were forbidden to speak their native languages.

Despite this **persecution**, many Native Americans clung on to their cultures through the first half of the twentieth century. The Society of American Indians was founded in 1911 and its

campaign for U.S. citizenship for Native Americans was successful in 1924. Other Native American organizations were formed to promote traditional cultures and to campaign politically for Native American rights.

This photo of a Sioux chief, Strike With Nose, was taken by Herman Heyn in 1899, when most of the Sioux people lived on reservations.

THE ROAD TO SELF-GOVERNMENT

Despite these campaigns, Native Americans on reservations endured poverty and very low standards of living. Many of them moved away to work and live in cities, where they hoped life would be better. In most cases, they found life just as difficult. They not only faced **discrimination** and **prejudice** but also could not compete successfully for jobs against whites and other more established ethnic groups.

In the 1970s, the American Indian Movement (AIM) organized large protests that attracted attention worldwide. They highlighted the problems of unemployment, discrimination, and poverty that Native Americans experienced in North America.

The AIM protests led to changes in policy. Some new laws protected the civil rights of Native Americans, while other laws allowed tribal governments to be formed. Every Sioux reservation has its own elected tribal council. Today tribal governments have a wide range of powers. They operate large businesses and run their own schools and health care.

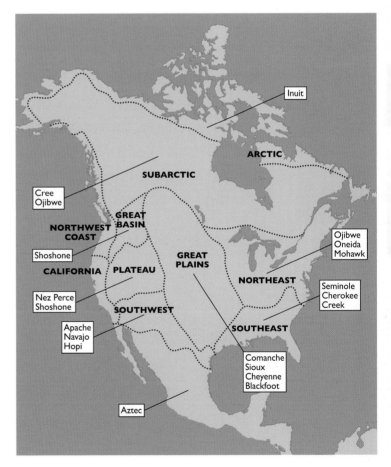

This map of North America highlights the main Native American cultural groups, along with the smaller groups, or tribes, featured in this series of books.

LAND AND ORIGINS

Chapter 1

SIOUX COUNTRY

The Sioux are one of the largest Native American nations, with a total population in the tens of thousands. Their homelands once covered the woodlands of the upper Mississippi River Valley, in what is now Minnesota, Wisconsin, Iowa, and Illinois. Today, they live on reservations in South and North Dakota, Minnesota, and Montana and throughout the United States and Canada.

FROM THE BLACK HILLS

No one knows exactly when the Sioux and other Native American tribes entered North America. Like most Native cultures, the Sioux have, for centuries, told an origin story that explains how they came to live here. According to the Sioux **elders**, they came from the Star Nation to a place beneath the earth and emerged from Wind Cave in the Black Hills of present-day South Dakota. The Black Hills, which they call *Paha Sapa,* "the heart of everything that is," are a sacred place for the Sioux people.

This map shows the Sioux groups and their movement from their former territories as they were pushed farther west.

French Creek winds its way through a meadow in the Black Hills. The Black Hills are a place of special **spiritual** significance not only to the Sioux but to other Plains tribes as well, including the Cheyennes.

THE SIOUX LANGUAGES

The Siouan language family is one of the most widely distributed throughout the eastern half of North America and includes tribes that are not called Sioux. Depending upon which of the three main dialects, or forms, of the language they speak, the Sioux call themselves Lakotas (also called the Tetons), Nakotas (or Yanktons), or Dakotas (or Santees). Each of the three main divisions of the Sioux nation includes a number of subtribes.

"Sioux" itself is a word from the **Ojibwe** language meaning "adders," a kind of poisonous snake. (The Sioux did not always get along well with their Ojibwe neighbors.)

Lakota Words

Lakota	Pronunciation	English
kola	ko-lah	friend
toka	toe-kah	enemy
wakan	wah-con	sacred
wi	we	sun
wicasa	we-kah-sah	man
sa	sah	red
mato	mah-toe	bear
wicoti	we-koh-tee	camp
hunka	hun-kah	parent
oyate	o-yah-tay	people
winyan	win-yon	woman

THE BEGINNING OF CONFLICT

The Sioux did not have much early contact with Europeans. By the late 1600s, however, the Ojibwes had traded with the French for guns, and they began using those weapons to push the Sioux tribes out of the woodlands of the upper Mississippi River Valley west onto the northern Great Plains.

The Lakota Sioux were pushed the farthest west, all the way to the plains in present-day Wyoming, western South Dakota, and western Nebraska. The Nakotas settled mostly on the northern plains in the present-day states of North and South Dakota. The Dakotas settled along the far western edge of their old homeland, mostly in present-day western Minnesota.

Nineteenth-century **media** depicted the West as wide-open spaces ripe for settlement, as shown in this 1861 painting *The Way of the Empire Is Going Westward*, by Emanuel Leutze. The European-Americans, however, found the land had long been inhabited by native peoples.

THE SETTLERS ARRIVE

In 1804, as Meriwether Lewis and William Clark began their journey of exploration across the continent, they visited some Lakota villages along the Missouri River. They were to be followed by many more Americans; between the 1840s and the completion of the **transcontinental** railroad in 1869, nearly 400,000 Americans passed through the southern edge of the Sioux country on the wagon trail to Utah and the West Coast known as the Oregon Trail. In a **treaty** with the United States in 1851, the Sioux agreed to allow the travelers to use the trail.

In 1854, however, a dispute over a cow that had wandered away from a wagon train caused a foolish young U.S. Army officer, Lieutenant John Grattan, to fire a cannon into a Lakota village, killing the village chief. The enraged Lakotas then killed the officer and all twenty-eight of his men. The next year, the army struck back by destroying a Lakota village, killing about seventy people.

In 1854, the Dakotas went to war against settlers who were taking their land in Minnesota. In 1862, when the long, bloody war was over, the United States government hanged thirty-eight Dakotas in the largest mass **execution** in U.S. history, and the Dakotas lost most of their Minnesota land.

Young Crazy Horse

A model of the Crazy Horse Memorial in front of the mountaintop in the Black Hills that is being carved in its likeness.

Among the Indians who witnessed the fight over the cow was a young Lakota who would later be known as Crazy Horse, one of the greatest Sioux military leaders. He was only about fourteen years old at the time, not yet a warrior, but the terrible event made a lasting impression on him. He never trusted the U.S. Army again.

WAR ON THE PLAINS

In the mid-1860s, gold seekers began streaming through the heart of Lakota country to get to a gold strike at present-day Bozeman, Montana. Over the protests of the Sioux, the U.S. Army built three forts along the Bozeman Trail to protect the miners. The Sioux went to war. Led by Red Cloud, they attacked the forts. A young war leader, Crazy Horse, gained fame in December 1866, when he trapped and killed a **cavalry** troop of about eighty men.

In 1868, under the Fort Laramie Treaty with the Sioux, the United States abandoned the three forts. The Sioux burned them down in a great victory celebration.

The 1868 Fort Laramie Treaty also stated that the Black Hills in South Dakota belonged to the Sioux. In 1874, however, the U.S. Army

Red Cloud led his people in wars against the Pawnees and Crows and battled the United States in the 1860s.

Lieutenant Colonel George Armstrong Custer's expedition into the Black Hills in 1874. Custer knew that he was **violating** the 1868 Fort Laramie treaty by entering the Black Hills without the permission of the Sioux, but he had no respect for the rights of the Indians.

A photo taken in 1879, of the Little Bighorn battle site, three years after Custer's defeat. Horse bones and boots are scattered on the hillside.

deliberately violated the treaty when Lieutenant Colonel George Custer confirmed rumors of gold in the Black Hills, starting a wild gold rush into the heart of the sacred land of the Sioux. The Sioux went to war again.

VICTORY AND DEFEAT

With their main leader Crazy Horse, the Sioux and their Cheyenne allies won a stunning victory at the Battle of the Rosebud against a large army. A few days later, on June 25, 1876, at the Battle of the Little Bighorn, they killed Lieutenant Colonel Custer and all of his men, stunning the nation.

The United States sent out large armies and within a year forced all of the Sioux and Cheyennes to surrender. Meanwhile, independent buffalo hunters, with the help of the U.S. Army, were **slaughtering** the buffalo herds for their hides. Without the animal they depended on, the Sioux lost much of their way of life and were forced to accept life on reservations mostly in North and South Dakota.

Crazy Horse rode up . . . [and said] "There's a good fight coming over the hill." I looked where he pointed and saw Custer and his bluecoats pouring over the hill. I thought there were a million of them. "That's where the big fight is going to be," said Crazy Horse. . . . He was not a bit excited. He made a joke of it.

Short Buffalo, Lakota

This Ghost Dance shirt was returned to the tribe in 1999 from a museum in Scotland.

THE GHOST DANCE

Despair at the misery of reservation life led the Sioux to embrace a new religion that swept through the reservations in 1890. The Ghost Dance religion was founded by a Paiute prophet named Wovoka. He preached that, if Indians embraced the Ghost Dance, the buffalo would return, along with all the dead Indians, and the white people would disappear.

On the Sioux reservations, some religious leaders said that special Ghost Dance shirts would protect them from bullets. The army became alarmed when the influential leader, Sitting Bull, embraced the new religion.

Sitting Bull

By 1857, when he was in his mid twenties, Sitting Bull was both a **medicine man** and a war chief. After helping to defeat Custer at the Battle of the Little Bighorn, Sitting Bull led his followers to Canada to avoid capture by the U.S. Army. Exhaustion and a lack of food forced him to surrender in 1881 at Fort Buford in Dakota Territory. In his later years, he strongly opposed government efforts to force the Sioux to adopt white values. He was killed during the army's attempt to arrest him.

U.S. soldiers picking up Lakotas killed at the massacre at Wounded Knee. The bodies, frozen in the deep winter cold, were buried in a mass grave.

WOUNDED KNEE, 1890

Ghost Dance followers gathered at a place called the Stronghold in the Black Hills. Big Foot, an **influential** chief who did not embrace the new religion, gathered his three hundred people and rushed across the Dakotas in the middle of winter toward the Stronghold to try to stop war from breaking out. He wanted to talk everyone into remaining calm.

The army, unaware that Big Foot was trying to encourage peace, sent troops to **intercept** him. Soldiers surrounded Big Foot's band in late December 1890 as they were camped along Wounded Knee Creek. When the army tried to take all the band's rifles, a gun went off. No one knows who fired the shot. The army fired its cannons, killing at least 150 of the mostly unarmed men, women, and children. The dead were buried in a mass grave, and the Sioux **reluctantly** resigned themselves to reservation life.

As part of the U.S. government's plan to make the Sioux adopt European-American ways, the Sioux were taught how to be farmers.

RESERVATION LIFE AND ACCULTURATION

Late-nineteenth-century Americans believed there was no place in their society for Indians to remain Indians — the reservation system was designed to force Indians to abandon their culture, language, religion, and **economy**. The government attempted to force them to adopt white values in a process called **acculturation**. It was a grim time for the Sioux.

People in the U.S. government who were supposed to help Native Americans did just the opposite. With the buffalo herds gone, the only food for the Sioux was what the U.S. government provided at the reservation, where the Indian agent was the government's official representative. Some Indian agents took money meant for food and offered cheap, spoiled beef and flour filled with insects to the people living on the Sioux reservations, pocketing the money they had saved.

> [The Sioux] understood that ample provisions would be made for their support; instead, their supplies have been reduced and much of the time they have been living on half and two-thirds rations.
>
> *General Nelson A. Miles, U.S. Army, 1891*

THE AMERICAN INDIAN MOVEMENT

The traditional Sioux ways of governing themselves were no longer allowed. Poverty, unemployment, poor health, and high death rates on the reservations made them islands of despair.

By the 1970s, Indians from across the country were determined to change the conditions on their reservations. A number of young Sioux became members of the American Indian Movement (AIM) and traveled to Washington, D.C., in what became known as "The Trail of Broken Treaties." They seized and occupied the headquarters of the Bureau of Indian Affairs, bringing media attention to Indian problems.

Similar events around the country forced the U.S government to take action. Particularly important were laws to allow Native Americans freedom of religion, which helped usher in a new era for the Sioux and other Indians.

The cruelest part of acculturation was the off-reservation boarding school system. Sioux children were taken by force from their families and sent to boarding schools. Forbidden to speak their language, they were forced to learn English.

TRADITIONAL WAY OF LIFE

A Plains Indian village on the move, using the travois, a horse-drawn sled. Moving an entire village was a great undertaking, requiring the help and cooperation of everyone.

A PEOPLE OF THE HORSE

After the Sioux acquired horses from other tribes (that had gotten them from the Spanish) during the 1700s, their world changed dramatically. Horses made travel easier. Before the horse, dogs had been used to drag tent poles and **tepees** across the plains. On a pole sled commonly known as a **travois**, horses could drag those items much farther and faster than dogs, and they could move much more weight. Entire villages of people and all their goods could be moved easily and quickly.

An Indian horse race. Horses had great value for Plains Indians, for recreation as well as transportation, war, and moving villages.

AN IMPROVING LIFESTYLE

Thanks to the horse, the Sioux's quality of life improved during the eighteenth century. Tepee poles could be longer, and the tepees bigger. Hunting buffalo became much easier and more efficient. Because food was easier to get, more babies lived to become adults. As both their ability to travel and their population increased, so did their power.

The era of warfare on foot gave way to one that produced some of the most spectacular light cavalry in history. Much of Sioux warfare, however, consisted simply of horse-stealing raids against other tribes. It was a way for young men to prove themselves and to gain wealth and honor within the tribe.

Lakotas on Horseback

The Lakotas, especially, took to the horse as if they had been born to ride. The traditional Indian style of child rearing, in which children are pretty much allowed to do whatever they think they can do, produced a culture where children barely more than toddlers performed breathtaking feats of horsemanship. By the time they were teens, they had amazing riding skills.

Horses, rifles, and pistols made it possible for the buffalo to be killed in great numbers. However, it was the coming of the railroads that made it possible for **commercial** hunters to hunt the buffalo nearly to extinction.

A PEOPLE OF THE BUFFALO

For the Sioux, especially the Lakotas, moving to the Great Plains made them a people of the buffalo, a great change from the woodland people they once had been. The Great Plains were home to immense herds of buffalo — at their greatest number estimated to be 75 million animals. The Plains also teemed with

many other kinds of animals, including elk and deer. It was a paradise for a people skilled at harvesting the plants and animals that lived around them.

The buffalo provided for nearly every Sioux need — not just for food, but for clothing and shelter as well. Buffalo robes warmed their beds on cold winter nights. Buffalo hides, stitched together with buffalo **sinew**, made a strong tent fabric, able to withstand rain and cold winter winds.

When draped around a framework of long, slender poles, the buffalo hides formed a tepee, a home that could be quickly put together or taken down and easily carried.

The Sioux fashioned buffalo horns into spoons and large bones into weapons. They cut tanned hides into thin strips and wound the strips into stout ropes. They made glue by boiling the hooves.

A buffalo hunt was an occasion for a great feast. One buffalo, weighing a ton or more, provided more fresh meat than could be eaten at one time. The remaining meat was cut into strips and dried in the sun, making a **jerky** that would last a long time.

The Slaughter of the Buffalo Herds

The end of the buffalo herds — within little more than a decade around the 1870s — came so suddenly as to stagger the imagination. The slaughter followed railroad building, offering hide hunters a means of transporting hides, which sold for about a dollar each back east. The hunters

Before the Plains Indians acquired horses, killing a buffalo was a difficult task. Getting close enough to a buffalo to kill it with an arrow required great skill.

took only the hides, leaving the meat to rot on the Plains. The U.S. Army encouraged the slaughter as one way of ending the Plains Indians' way of life and forcing them onto the reservation.

The slaughter began in Kansas in the early 1870s, wiping out the herds there by 1873. By 1875, the Texas herds had been killed. The railroads reached Montana in 1871, and by 1875, the northern herds were gone. With the slaughter of the buffalo herds, the Plains Indian way of life disappeared.

TRIBAL LEADERS

In the era of the buffalo, during the seventeenth and eighteenth centuries, the basic unit of Sioux political organization was the *tiyospaye*. Each tiyospaye consisted of about thirty or more households of related families. The families of the tiyospaye traveled together, hunted together, and spent the entire year together. At intervals, all of the many tiyospayes in the tribe would come together for a large meeting of the entire tribe.

A nineteenth-century painting by Seth Eastman showing Sioux men in council. The Sioux place great value on the wisdom of their elders, and their traditional government is designed to allow the people to be guided by that wisdom.

Each tiyospaye had a headman who achieved and kept his position by virtue of his character. He could lose that position by making foolish decisions, putting the group in danger, or failing to live up to the high standards expected of him. While he was not elected, the people had to agree to let him lead.

The most able and respected headmen from the tiyospayes were admitted into male societies called *nacas*. The most important of these societies was called the *Naca Omincia*, which was very much like a national council, having the power to make war and peace. From among its members, *wicasa itancans* (executive officers) were appointed to carry out the decisions of the Naca Omincia.

The *wicasa wakan*, or medicine man, holds a special place in traditional Sioux life, both historically and today. He is a healer, respected for his power to cure, as well as a wise leader.

Today, large extended families still have leaders among them who act as an informal kind of traditional Sioux government. This form of government is not recognized by the United States government, and that causes many of the problems between the U.S. government and the Sioux today — and even among the Sioux themselves, between those people who follow the old ways and those who don't.

The Qualities of a Leader

Traditionally, people have become leaders among the Sioux by having characteristics that are valued by the community. These include wisdom, courage, generosity, compassion for the needs of others, and an ability to gain spiritual guidance from dreams and visions.

An Oglala Sioux man visiting Bear Butte, in the Black Hills, a holy site for the Sioux. The prayer ribbons on the trees represent religious commitments made by the visitors to the **sacred** ground.

BELIEFS AND VALUES

Sioux traditional religious beliefs remain strong, even today. Traditionally, the Sioux believe in a Creator, sometimes called the Great Mystery.

They believe that the Great Mystery is present in all things on the earth, including the rocks, trees, animals, water and wind. They seek guidance from the Creator in dreams and visions. They also place great importance on trying to live in harmony with other people. Medicine men help **interpret** the dreams and visions.

For the Sioux, Bear Butte in the Black Hills is a place for fasting and praying, somewhere to seek a vision to guide one's life. Unfortunately, Bear Butte is now controlled by the U.S. government. The Sioux must pay fees to the U.S. park rangers to enter Bear Butte. Tourists often show little respect for the prayer ribbons that the Sioux tie to the bushes and the tobacco offerings to the Creator that they leave on the butte. Tobacco is a sacred plant, used in prayers and ceremonies.

THE SUN DANCE

The most important religious ceremony, the Sun Dance is held each year in the summer. The ceremonies help the **participants** cleanse their spirits and renew their vows to work for the welfare of the Sioux tribe.

Sioux traditional values emphasize the welfare of the group rather than the individual. Sharing and having concern for others are highly valued. **Hoarding** wealth, by not sharing with others, is frowned upon.

THE SIOUX COMMUNITY

The Sioux may be poor, in terms of money, but they share that condition of poverty together. The Sioux value a rich and rewarding family life with their relatives throughout the entire community more than trying to make money.

Sioux contentment with this outlook on life and their sense of what is important and what is not important are a measure of how successful they have been at surviving an era when their culture was under threat of extinction.

Sioux performers of the Eagle Dance. Traditional Sioux dances and ceremonies were banned for many years by the U.S. government in its attempt to force the Sioux to adopt white values.

Iktomi the Trickster

Many Sioux stories feature a character called Iktomi, which means "spider." Despite his name, Iktomi is a human figure, a man who is selfish and greedy, and who is often punished for his bad behavior.

Iktomi was foolish because he did not realize that muskrats are perfectly at home in the water. In fact, muskrats can swim around underwater for around fifteen minutes without coming to the surface to breathe.

IKTOMI AND THE MUSKRAT

One day as Iktomi was cooking fish soup by a lake, Muskrat appeared. It was a Sioux custom to offer to share food with visitors, so Muskrat waited to be offered some food. But Iktomi was not a generous man. After a while he said he would share the food if Muskrat could beat him in a race round the lake. Muskrat agreed, but only if Iktomi would carry a heavy stone as he ran.

They walked to the opposite side of the lake and then set off in different directions. After a while, Iktomi realized he could not see any grass moving where Muskrat should have been, so he dropped the stone and ran faster.

When Iktomi reached his camp, he found the soup had gone. He realized that Muskrat must have swum across the lake and taken the soup. Then he saw Muskrat in a tree above him, finishing his meal. Iktomi was now very hungry and begged for something to eat. Muskrat dropped a sharp bone, which fell straight into Iktomi's throat, making him choke. Then Iktomi wished that he had offered to share his meal with Muskrat in the beginning and not been so selfish.

The peacock is a very beautiful bird, but its magnificent feathers are not suited for flight. Iktomi wanted to look like a peacock, but he was not content with the peacock's ground-based lifestyle.

IKTOMI AND THE PEACOCK

On another occasion, Iktomi saw Peacock and wanted the same beautiful feathers for himself. Peacock could work magic, and he offered to turn Iktomi into a peacock but only on one condition. Iktomi agreed to do anything, and so he became a peacock.

After sitting in a tree for a while, Iktomi suddenly decided that he wanted to fly off into the sky with the other birds. Peacock told him if he wanted to remain a peacock, the one condition was that he did not try to fly like other birds.

Iktomi, of course, did not listen and lunged into the air. Instantly, he fell to the ground and was a man again. But he never learned a lesson from this experience, and he continued to want to be things he was not.

SIOUX LIFE TODAY

THE CONTEMPORARY SIOUX

Sixteen Sioux reservations lie in the United States. Other Sioux people live in the Prairie Provinces of Canada. Today, about half the Sioux live on the reservations; most of the others live in large cities. Land area, population, tribal divisions represented, natural resources, and economic conditions all vary greatly among the Sioux reservations. An elected tribal council governs each reservation.

RESERVATION LIFE

Life on most of the reservations is difficult, with many people lacking jobs. Poverty and despair have led to alcohol abuse and poor health. These problems brought violence to the Pine Ridge Reservation in the 1970s, from which the Sioux are still recovering. It was a struggle over which group would control the reservation — the Sioux who want to follow the old ways or the Sioux who have adopted nonnative values. Nearly one hundred traditional Sioux people were killed in the violence. The struggle between those two groups continues today, but it is no longer marked by the violence that made the reservation a dangerous place in the 1970s.

Sioux reservations of various sizes are scattered throughout Minnesota, Montana, and North and South Dakota.

These conflicts brought media attention to Indian problems and helped change U.S. policy. Instead of trying to force Indians to give up their cultures, the government sought ways to allow Indians to have more control over their own lives.

EMPLOYMENT

There is very little industry on Sioux reservations because they are located in areas far from big manufacturing centers. Large numbers of Sioux people on the reservations work for U.S. government agencies and programs. Many others work in cattle ranching and mining.

Wounded Knee, 1973

For more than two months in 1973, the American Indian Movement (AIM) occupied the church at Wounded Knee, South Dakota, on the Pine Ridge Reservation, the scene of the 1890 massacre. AIM members held it as the center of an Indian nation — independent of the U.S. government — for seventy-one days. The incident deepened the divisions among the Sioux at Pine Ridge that caused several years of violence over who would control the reservation and speak for the Lakota Sioux tribe.

March 3, 1973, a U.S. flag flies upside down outside Wounded Knee church, on the Pine Ridge Reservation in South Dakota. An upside-down flag is a signal of distress.

EDUCATION PROBLEMS

Fewer than one quarter of Sioux children graduate from high school, and only 17 percent of graduates go on to colleges. Reasons for this are a lack of funding for education and for transport to school, and too few jobs available for young people after they leave school.

At a meeting in South Dakota in 2010, many Sioux teachers gave evidence of the difficulties they faced. These problems include crumbling, and even unsafe, school buildings, lack of teaching materials and books, lack of heating and air conditioning, and few good teachers. The teachers wanted better funding for education and more tribal control over what children are taught.

Also in 2010, Keith Moore of the Rosebud Sioux tribe was appointed director of the federal Bureau of Indian Education, which funds schools on the reservations.

Three-year-old Dakota children at a day care center today. They are sitting in front of a mural that depicts scenes from traditional Dakota life.

The hoop dance, which uses 28 hoops, depicts life emerging in spring from the darkness of winter.

VISUAL AND PERFORMING ARTS

Sioux visual and performing artists, authors, and scholars have been leaders in the **intellectual** and cultural life of American Indians. In the visual and performing arts, Oscar Howe (1915–1984), from the Crow Creek Reservation, became one of the best-known Indian artists in North America. For many years, he was a professor of arts at the University of South Dakota. Today, his work, which features images of changing native culture, is a part of the permanent collection of many American museums.

Kevin Locke, from the Standing Rock Reservation, is famous nationally as an Indian flute player and hoop dancer. He is also the founder of the Kevin Locke Native Dance Ensemble, a group of dancers, musicians, and storytellers from several Native American tribes.

Kevin Locke plays the traditional cedar wood flute of the Northern Plains.

Another Sioux musician, Floyd Red Crow Westerman (1936–2007), was a country music singer who made many recordings. He became an actor in 1989 and appeared in many movies, including *Dances With Wolves* (1990), and on television, including in *The X-Files*.

SIOUX AUTHORS AND SCHOLARS

Sioux authors have also made important contributions to children's literature. The most acclaimed author, Virginia Driving Hawk Sneve, from the Rosebud Reservation, won the 1992 North American Indian Prose Award. As well as many children's books, she has also written history books for adults. *Completing the Circle* (1995) traces the histories of her female ancestors.

Vine Deloria, Jr., (1933–2005), from the Standing Rock Reservation, was easily the best-known Sioux author. He held graduate degrees in both law and religious studies. He gained national attention in 1969 with his first book, *Custer Died for Your Sins,* which was published while he was still a student in law school. He published many other influential books, including *Red Earth, White Lies* (1995). This book criticizes scientific **theories** about how native peoples came to the Americas, partly because these theories do not take into account native origin stories.

Tiffany Midge is one of the most promising Sioux poets and activists. Her work has been honored by other writers.

This Oglala College student celebrates her Sioux heritage at a powwow on the Pine Ridge Reservation in South Dakota.

The Sioux also have many other authors who publish poetry or fiction. Their work is widely used in college courses in Native American literature.

Susan Power is a Standing Rock Sioux. Her first novel was *The Grass Dancer* (1994), about four generations of a Native American family, covering more than a hundred years. Robert L. Perea is part Oglala Sioux. He teaches philosophy and history in Phoenix, Arizona. Perea has published many short stories, including the award-winning *Stacey's Story*. Philip H. Red-Eagle, Jr., is of part Dakota, part Salish descent. His novel *Red Earth* (1997) is based on his experiences in the Vietnam War. Elizabeth Cook-Lynn was born on the Crow Creek Reservation. She was a professor of English and Native American Studies at Eastern Washington University, as well as an author and poet. Her books present a Native American view of American history.

CURRENT SIOUX ISSUES

In the 1980s, when former professional basketball player Bill Bradley was a United States senator from New Jersey, he conducted a basketball camp one summer for Sioux children on the Pine Ridge Reservation. Seeing their poverty, Senator Bradley asked the children what he could do in the Senate to help them. He was surprised when the children told him that the thing they wanted the most was for the United States to return Paha Sapa (the Black Hills) to them.

VICTORY, OF A SORT

To the Sioux, the Black Hills are their most sacred land. In the twentieth century, they went to court against the U.S. government to have them returned to their care.

Sioux children jumping on a trampoline. Sioux children, like children everywhere, just want to have fun.

In proceedings before the U.S. Indian Claims Commission, the Sioux won a decision that the Black Hills had been taken from them illegally. In 1980, however, the Supreme Court ruled that the Sioux were only entitled to money — a $122 million award — not the land itself.

A Sacred Land

The 1993 HBO video *Paha Sapa: The Struggle for the Black Hills* features interviews with many Sioux and Cheyenne leaders, including young people, about the importance of the Black Hills as sacred land to their people. The video shows the pollution of the region by uranium mining and timber companies. It also draws a sharp contrast between the Sioux reverence for the land and such commercial uses of it as building the gambling town of Deadwood into a commercial tourist attraction and carving the images of U.S. presidents onto **Mount Rushmore**.

On Mount Rushmore, Lakota Indians protest the United States' offer of money in return for ownership of the Black Hills.

Russell Means

In the 1970s, Russell Means was one of the most active Sioux members of the American Indian Movement. He was a spokesperson for AIM when the activist organization took over the church at Wounded Knee in 1973. In the 1990s, he became a Hollywood actor, starring in major motion pictures. He is best known for his role in the movie *Last Of The Mohicans* but continues to be active in Native political issues.

In 2007, Means was the leader of a group of Sioux activists who called themselves the Lakota Freedom Delegation. They declared Lakotah (all the traditional homelands of the Lakota people) a self-governing nation, independent from the United States. They also rejected all previous treaties between the Sioux and the U.S. government. These actions have not been backed by tribal councils on the Sioux reservations.

In 2008, Russell Means ran for presidency of the Oglala Lakota but was narrowly defeated.

Russell Means speaks to supporters before beginning his walk across New Mexico in his campaign for governor in 2002.

American Indian Movement (AIM) activists Dennis Banks, left, and Clyde Bellecourt beat a drum and chant during a rally at the Pine Ridge Reservation in South Dakota.

The Sioux have refused to take the money, which has now increased to more than $400 million. They continue to demand that the Black Hills be returned to them.

They point to previous cases. In the 1970s, Congress passed legislation, signed by President Richard Nixon, that returned the sacred Blue Lake to Taos Pueblo in New Mexico, along with 48,000 acres (19,433 ha) of surrounding land.

Presently, the only way the Black Hills can be returned to the Sioux is by an act of Congress. In the 1980s, legislation to that effect, sponsored by Senator Bradley, came very close to passing in Congress. The Sioux are not losing faith and continue trying to convince Congress to pass that legislation.

Today, in the twenty-first century, the Sioux people still face many problems. But they have also produced many capable leaders who are working hard to solve those problems and to continue their heritage as one of the great Indian nations.

TIMELINE

1600	Ojibwes acquire guns and push the Sioux west to the Great Plains in present-day Wyoming, Nebraska, North and South Dakota, and western Minnesota.
1640	Sioux meet French explorers near the headwaters of the Mississippi River.
about 1730	Sioux acquire horses from other tribes.
1760s	Lakota Sioux people reach the Black Hills.
1804	Lewis and Clark expedition visits Sioux villages.
1840–1869	Thousands of Americans pass through Sioux country on the Oregon Trail.
1851	Sioux give up most of their territory in Minnesota and relocate to reservations along the Minnesota River; Lakota Sioux sign treaty allowing travelers to use the Oregon Trail.
1854	Dispute over a cow leads to violent clash with U.S. Army.
1855	Army strikes back by destroying a Sioux village.
1862	Sioux uprising ends in defeat with the hanging of thirty-eight Dakotas.
mid-1860s	Gold seekers cross through Lakota Sioux country to Bozeman, Montana; U.S. Army builds three forts on Sioux land; Sioux attack the forts and kill a cavalry troop.
1868	Treaty of Fort Laramie; United States abandons the forts.
1874	Custer leads U.S. troops exploring for gold in Black Hills.
1876	Sioux and Cheyenne win victories over the U.S. Army at the Battle of the Rosebud and the Battle of the Little Bighorn.
1877	Crazy Horse killed. Sioux and Cheyenne surrender.

1890   Sioux embrace the Ghost Dance religion; Sitting Bull killed; massacre at Wounded Knee.

1800s   Extinction of the buffalo drives Sioux onto reservations in the
and 1900s   Dakotas; despair on reservations over U.S. government policy of acculturation and the off-reservation boarding-school system.

1973   American Indian Movement occupies a church at Wounded Knee for seventy-one days.

1974   U.S. Indian Claims Commission awards $122 million to the Sioux Nation for illegal taking of the Black Hills; the Sioux refuse to take the money.

1980   U.S. Supreme Court upholds U.S. Indian Claims Commission money award to the Sioux.

1985   Senator Bill Bradley introduces a bill to give the Black Hills back to the Sioux Nation in the U.S. Senate; Representative James Howard introduces a similar bill in the U.S. House of Representatives. Both bills are voted down.

2007   Lakota Freedom Delegation, a group of Sioux activists led by Russell Means, declares independence from the United States, withdraws from all treaties and declares Lakotah a sovereign nation; Lakota elected tribal councils do not give their support.

2008   Russell Means runs for presidency of the Oglala Lakota and is narrowly defeated.

2010   Sioux teachers highlight lack of money available for education and school buildings; Keith Moore, Rosebud Sioux, is appointed director of the federal Bureau of Indian Education.

GLOSSARY

acculturation: the process of forcing one group to adopt the culture — the language, lifestyle, and values — of another.

ancestors: people from whom an individual or group is descended.

boarding schools: places where students must live at the school.

cavalry: warriors or soldiers trained to fight on horseback.

commercial: concerned with making money.

culture: the arts, beliefs, and customs that make up a people's way of life.

discrimination: unjust treatment, usually because of a person's race or sex.

economy: the way a country or people produces, divides up, and uses its goods and money.

elder: a tribal leader.

environment: objects and conditions all around that affect living things and communities.

execution: the killing of someone by a government or as a political act.

floodplain: the area of land beside a river or stream that is covered with water during a flood.

hoarding: keeping something for yourself and not sharing it with others.

ice age: a period of time when the earth is very cold and lots of water in the oceans turns to ice.

influential: being able to affect what other people do or say.

intellectual: concerned with use of thinking and reasoning.

intercept: prevent someone going somewhere.

interpret: explain the meaning of words, a language, or actions.

irrigation: any system for watering the land to grow plants.

jerky: thin strips of meat, dried in the sun, until most of their moisture is removed.

media: television, radio, newspapers, the Internet, and other forms of communication.

medicine man: a spiritual or religious leader.

migration: movement from one place to another.

Mount Rushmore: a monument in the Black Hills featuring large stone carvings of four U.S. presidents.

Ojibwe: also known as Chippewa or Anishinabe (their own name for themselves).

participant: a person taking part.

persecution: treating someone or a certain group of people badly over a period of time.

prejudice: dislike or injustice that is not based on reason or experience.

reluctantly: unwillingly.

reservation: land set aside by the U.S. government for specific Native American tribes to live on.

sacred: set apart for religious purposes.

sinew: tendon, a tough, fibrous tissue used for sewing thread.

slaughter: killing, especially in large numbers.

spiritual: affecting the human spirit or religion rather than physical things.

tepee: a cone-shaped tent supported by long, slender pine poles and draped with buffalo hides.

theory: a group of ideas that explain something.

transcontinental: crossing a continent.

travois: a sled consisting of two poles pulled across the ground.

treaty: an agreement among two or more peoples or nations.

violate: treat with disrespect or break an agreement.

MORE RESOURCES

WEBSITES:

http://www.bigorrin.org/sioux_kids.htm
Online Sioux Indian Fact Sheet For Kids in question and answer form with useful links.

http://www.brooklynmuseum.org/opencollection/artists /719/Sioux_Native_American
Photos of historic Sioux clothing and artifacts from the Brooklyn Museum.

www.lakhota.org/ALPHABET/alphabet.htm
This website gives examples of letters, pronunciations, meanings, and audio samples of various Lakota words.

http://www.native-languages.org/dakota.htm
A guide to the Dakota-Lakota language, including vocabulary.

http://www.native-languages.org/sioux-legends.htm
A brief description of Sioux mythological figures plus many links to Sioux legends and traditional stories and to books on Sioux mythology.

http://www.pbs.org/weta/thewest/program/
The New Perspectives on the West pages contain information about Sioux leaders, events, and issues.

http://www.sacredland.org/black-hills/
This page in the Sacred Lands Film Project explores the history of and issues surrounding the conflict over the Black Hills area.

http://www.woundedkneemuseum.org/main_menu.html
The Wounded Knee Museum website explores the background and events leading up to the Wounded Knee massacre.

DVD:

Incident at Oglala: The Leonard Peltier Story. Lion Gate, 2004.

Books:

Burgan, Michael. *The Lakota (First Americans).* Marshall Cavendish Children's Books, 2008.

Cunningham, Kevin, and Peter Benoit. *The Sioux (True Books).* Children's Press, 2011.

Englar, Mary. *The Sioux and Their History (We the People).* Compass Point Books, 2005.

Gibson, Karen Bush. *Native American History for Kids: With 21 Activities.* Chicago Review Press, 2010.

Haugen, Brenda. *Crazy Horse: Sioux Warrior (Signature Lives: American Frontier Era Series).* Compass Point Books, 2006.

Jeffrey, Gary. *Sitting Bull: The Life of a Lakota Chief.* Rosen Publishing Group, 2005.

King, David C. *First People.* DK Children, 2008.

Koopmans, Anna. *The Sioux (American Indian Art and Culture).* Chelsea House Publications, 2004.

Lavine, Michelle. *The Sioux (Native American Histories).* Lerner Classroom, 2007.

Murdoch, David S. *North American Indian (DK Eyewitness Books).* DK Children, 2005.

Nelson, S. D. *Black Elk's Vision: A Lakota Story.* Abrams Books for Young Readers, 2010.

Sneve, Virginia Driving Hawk. *Bad River Boys: A Meeting of the Lakota Sioux with Lewis and Clark.* Holiday House, 2005.

Sneve, Virginia Driving Hawk. *Lana's Lakota Moons.* Bison Books, 2007.

Stanley, George Edward. *Crazy Horse: Young War Chief (Childhood of Famous Americans).* Aladdin, 2005.

Stanley, George Edward. *Sitting Bull: Great Sioux Hero (Sterling Biographies).* Sterling, 2010.

Stein, R. Conrad. *The Sioux: A Proud People (American Indians).* Enslow Elementary, 2005.

Swain, Gwenyth. *Little Crow: Leader of the Dakota.* Borealis Books, 2004.

THINGS TO THINK ABOUT AND DO

WHAT DIFFERENCE DO HORSES MAKE?

Draw pictures showing how life would be for the Sioux on the buffalo plains both before and after they acquired horses. What would a buffalo hunt look like with horses and without them? How would moving a village from one camp to another look different?

WHAT SHOULD BE DONE ABOUT THE BLACK HILLS?

The U.S. Indian Claims Commission ruled that the United States took the Black Hills from the Sioux illegally. What do you think the United States should do about the Black Hills? Should U.S. citizens today feel responsible for things the government did in the past? How should future generations try to solve problems from the past? Write an essay with your thoughts.

DRAWING DAILY LIFE

Draw pictures showing all of the things the Sioux were able to make from a buffalo for use in their daily life. Decorate the tepees and clothing with painted symbols, beads, and porcupine quills. Look at the photos in this book for ideas about how to decorate the items.

INDEX